THE GREATEST FAITH EVER

Published by Aponet
in association with Covenant Publishing
ISBN: 978-87-91236-21-1

Contact: adeolushola@gmail.com

ACKNOWLEDGMENTS

I give praise to the incomparable, the only wise and the Almighty God for His grace and guidance in putting this book together.

I want to appreciate my beloved wife, Abiola and my lovely children, Grace-Anne and Theodora for your love and patience while I was putting this project together.

Tributes to the General Overseer of RCCG Worldwide, Pastor and Pastor Mrs E.A. Adeboye (Daddy and Mummy GO), you are highly appreciated.

Special thanks to all RCCG Pastors and Ministers all over the world.

CONTENTS

INTRODUCTION

One might think that great faith should have emerged from one of the great leaders of the day, such as the Scribes or Pharisees. As a matter of fact, Jesus sincerely desired for the Jews, His own people to demonstrate faith at a notable level but the scriptures introduced us to one who was not a Jew, but a gentile and also a soldier of the Roman army.

Ironic as it may seem, it isn't always the theologians who experience monumental breakthrough in spiritual things. Often, it is the housewife, the miner, the naval officer or other humble, common people who demonstrate great faith in God. We must never lose sight that the Gospel is a simple message which has no respect of persons, nor requires any special credentials for it to be believed.

The greatest faith in the world is to wholly trust upon the Word of God, that is, to take God at His Word.

Faith knocks down barriers without touching them.

Hebrews 11: 30 says,

By faith the walls of Jericho fell down after they were encircled for seven days.

Faith passes through the places the faithless cannot go.

Hebrews 11:29 says,

By faith they passed through the Red Sea as by dry land, whereas the Egyptians, attempting to do so, were drowned.

Faith is putting all your eggs in God's basket, and then counting your blessings before they hatch."

Ramona C. Carroll.

CHAPTER ONE

THE SPIRIT OF FAITH

There is a human faith that is inborn within every person. Assuming you were told something was impossible for you to accomplish, but you accomplished it anyway because you believed you could. That was made possible because of your natural human faith.

The human faith can get some things done but it is based on and limited to the five physical senses- What one can see, taste, hear, smell, or feel. By natural human faith I entrust the contents of an envelope into the hands of postmen so that I may communicate with my friends in other countries. One can also embark a plane believing that the pilot and his crew are competent to take us to the desired destination.

However, what if you were asked to lie on a bed you couldn't see? With the human faith, your senses would have a problem with that.

Simply put there are things you cannot believe for without the supernatural God-kind of faith. You can't believe in invisible things with human faith. Many people are trying to believe God with their human faith. It will not work.

But Thomas, one of the twelve, called Didymus, was not with them when Jesus came.

The other disciples therefore said unto him, We have seen the LORD. But he said unto them, Except I shall see in his hands the print of the nails, and put my finger into the print of the nails, and thrust my hand into his side, I will not believe.

John 20:24-25

Notice Thomas said ...***Except I shall see in his hands the print of the nails, and put my finger into the print of the nails, and thrust my hand into his side, I will not believe.***

His faith was based on what he could see, **Except I**

shall see and what he could feel, ***put my finger into the print of the nails***, this is the human faith. God-kind of faith will believe without seeing.

The Lord Jesus did not commend Thomas's faith.

Jesus saith unto him, Thomas, because thou hast seen me, thou hast believed: blessed are they that have not seen, and yet have believed.

John 20:29

Many people want to see like Thomas before they believe, but spiritual blessings are conferred on those that will dare believe before they see or feel etc. Faith (God's kind) is a precursor to the blessings of God.

That the trial of your faith, being much more precious than of gold that perisheth, though it be tried with fire, might be found unto praise and honour and glory at the appearing of Jesus Christ:

Whom having not seen, ye love; in whom, though now ye see him not, yet believing, ye rejoice with joy unspeakable and full of glory:

1 Peter 1:7-8

Peter again commends the faith of the Jews going through trials. He was privileged to see Jesus but they did not yet they believed on him.

Whom having not seen, ye love; in whom, though now ye see him not, yet believing,

Notice further that their faith will be rewarded.

Faith is the key ingredient to life. It affects everything we think, say and do. It is a daily necessity, as the Scriptures says in 2 Corinthians 5:7 ***For we walk by faith, not by sight.***

Let us examine the story of these three students.

There was a schoolteacher who gave to three of his students a difficult problem. "You will find it very hard to solve," he said, "but there is a way." After repeated attempts, one of them gave up in despair. "There is no way!" he declared.

The second pupil had not succeeded, yet he was smiling and unconcerned. "I know it can be explained, because I have seen it done." he said.

The third worked on, long after the rest had given

up. His head ached and his brain was in a whirl. Yet as he went over it again and again, he said without faltering, "I know there is a way, because the teacher has said it."

Here is faith - that confidence that rests not upon what he has seen, but upon the promises or statement of another.

We can and should trust in God and in His Holy Word.

Natural human faith can accomplish a lot of things, but some things are just impossible by it.

For example, It is impossible for man to save himself. It is also impossible for man to heal himself of an incurable disease. A higher level of faith is needed for such. Only the supernatural God-kind of faith can do these things. This God-kind of faith is available to those who come to Christ and accept Him as their savior.

For by grace are ye saved through faith; and that not of yourselves: it is the gift of God:

Ephesians 2:8

In Mark 11:14, Jesus had just cursed a fig tree. He had wanted to eat from it, but arrived there to find no fruit on it. He proceeded to curse the fig tree. Let us examine what took place thereafter the next morning,

And Peter calling to remembrance saith unto him, Master, behold, the fig tree which thou cursedst is withered away.

And Jesus answering saith unto them, Have faith in God.

For verily I say unto you, That whosoever shall say unto this mountain, Be thou removed, and be thou cast into the sea; and shall not doubt in his heart, but shall believe that those things which he saith shall come to pass; he shall have whatsoever he saith.

Mark 11:21-23

Notice in verse 22, Jesus said to them in response to Peter's exclamation ...**Have faith in God.** In other words faith in God will get the result He got. A close look at verse 23 reveals how faith works.

Jesus says you can speak to your mountain believing that the things you say shall come to pass. In other words **"faith in God speaks what he believes"**

What is it that you believe God for? If God has promised healing, deliverance or prosperity in His word, you can believe for them and apply your faith accordingly.

Apostle Paul mentions the spirit of faith:

We having the same spirit of faith, according as it is written, I believed, and therefore have I spoken; we also believe, and therefore speak;

2 Corinthians 4:13

The Word of God tells us that "we have the same spirit of faith." Someone said "The principles of faith are taught, but the spirit of faith is caught" The spirit of faith calls things that be not as if they were.

The spirit of faith does exactly what God did in creation.

Through faith we understand that the worlds were

framed by the word of God, so that things which are seen were not made of things which do appear.

Hebrews 11:3

See that God is a faith God. We are told from the above scriptures that the worlds were framed by the word of God spoken by God in faith.

We read how God called things to be in Genesis 1:3, **And God said, Let there be light: and there was light.** God simply spoke what He believed into existence.

God expects all his children to live by faith. When you are challenged in life, release faith filled words of the living God into the situation and you will end up having whatever you say. You need not understand how these things will be but you can in the spirit of faith speak every promise of God into existence in your life.

CHAPTER TWO

EXAMINE YOUR FAITH WALK

I have often encountered people who claim to have faith only to discover upon close examination that they actually do not understand what faith is or how faith works. The answer in this case is beautifully expressed in my book- **THE SAYING PRINCIPLE.** I have equally met with people who genuinely believe that they do not, and cannot have faith enough to surmount the kind of problems they are faced with. I will again try to answer that as we read along in this chapter.

Furthermore, I am deeply concerned that the understanding of many believers regarding the word "faith" ends with the word "THE CHRISTIAN FAITH". Faith in a way can be referred to as belief in the traditional doctrines of a religion. Christianity is often referred to as the "Christian Faith". This refers to the whole spiritual realm of Christianity. Again faith is also defined as absolute confidence in God, His ability and/or His promises. Hebrews 11:1 says it this way:

Now faith is the substance of things hoped for, the evidence of things not seen.

There is need to distinguish between these two different meanings of faith. Faith goes beyond a mere reference to a religion.

This chapter is targeted at helping you identify the different expressions of faith that may apply to believers at different stages of their lives and how to keep developing in faith. It is possible to walk in great faith in one area of one's life and be weak or exercise no faith at all in another area.

WHERE ARE YOU IN YOUR FAITH WALK?

Throughout the scriptures you will find references depicting various levels of faith. The bible talks about weak and strong faith, little and great faith, full of faith and no faith, perfect faith, shipwrecked faith, dead faith etc.

Let us examine some of these different levels of faith:

NO FAITH

And he was in the hinder part of the ship, asleep on a pillow: and they awake him, and say unto him, Master, carest thou not that we perish?

And he arose, and rebuked the wind, and said unto the sea, Peace, be still. And the wind ceased, and there was a great calm.

And he said unto them, Why are ye so fearful? how is it that ye have no faith?

And they feared exceedingly, and said one to another, What manner of man is this, that even the wind and the sea obey him?

Mark 4:38-41

One of the most damaging and frequently used arrows of the enemy is fear. Fear when allowed, will always paralyze the activity of faith. Notice that the Lord actually expected them to take charge of the situation: *...**how is it that ye have no faith?*** Luke's account had it as "where is your faith?" Giving in to fear can render you inactive in the face of an attacker even if you are holding a gun in your hand. The disciples were not just afraid, they were full of fear and this totally paralyzed the activity of faith in them. Let us ensure we resist every invasion of fear as we learn to demonstrate our faith in the face of opposition or an impending danger.

SHIPWRECKED FAITH

This charge I commit unto thee, son Timothy, according to the prophecies which went before on thee, that thou by them mightest war a good warfare;

Holding faith, and a good conscience; which some having put away concerning faith have made shipwreck:

Of whom is Hymenaeus and Alexander; whom I have delivered unto Satan, that they may learn not to blaspheme.

1 Timothy 1:18-20

The mystery of faith is based on a pure conscience. Faith will fail when this is compromised. Our conscience must be void of offence; it must never be corrupted or overtaken by sin. This is a serious battle and every believer must engage therein. The battle of the conscience determines how far we go in life. The primary symptom of a faith headed for shipwreck is that good conscience is first set aside.

DEAD FAITH

What doth it profit, my brethren, though a man say he hath faith, and have not works? can faith save him?

If a brother or sister be naked, and destitute of daily food,

And one of you say unto them, Depart in peace, be ye warmed and filled; notwithstanding ye give them not those things which are needful to the body; what doth it profit?

Even so faith, if it hath not works, is dead, being alone.

James 2:15-17

Dead faith is simply faith without corresponding actions. We will learn more on this subject in chapter four. Dead faith yields no fruit and gives no profit.

PERFECT FAITH

Was not Abraham our father justified by works, when he had offered Isaac his son upon the altar?

Seest thou how faith wrought with his works, and by works was faith made perfect?

James 2:21-22

Again, exactly what dead faith ignored is what perfect faith employs in order to achieve excellence. It recognizes the importance of corresponding action to finish its course.

WEAK FAITH

Weak faith is found where faith is not well rooted in the word of God. It is rather distracted by physical evidence.

And being not weak in faith, he considered not his own body now dead, when he was about an hundred years old, neither yet the deadness of Sarah's womb:

Romans 4:19

To be weak in faith means to consider the evidence available contradicting the desired result. Medically speaking, Abraham and Sarah were not qualified to have children. The bible says his body was dead and Sarah's womb was equally dead. We must realize that it is weakness of faith that makes us consider or brood over the challenges in the way of our expectations from God. It may of course be intellectually correct, yet it is a breach on the operation of faith to regard the facts that arise against the fulfillment of God's promise.

STRONG FAITH

He staggered not at the promise of God through unbelief; but was strong in faith, giving glory to God;

Romans 4:19:20

Strong faith continues to give glory to God in spite of the evidence contradicting the desired result. Giving glory to God in faith affirms God's faithfulness ability and power. It simply brings honour to God.

LITTLE FAITH

Little faith means there is faith, but it lasts only for a while. Little faith began a journey but could not complete it. The little faith begins the journey with great zeal:

And in the fourth watch of the night Jesus went unto them, walking on the sea.

And when the disciples saw him walking on the sea, they were troubled, saying, It is a spirit; and they cried out for fear.

But straightway Jesus spake unto them, saying, Be of good cheer; it is I; be not afraid.

And Peter answered him and said, Lord, if it be thou, bid me come unto thee on the water.

And he said, Come. And when Peter was come down out of the ship, he walked on the water, to go to Jesus.

But when he saw the wind boisterous, he was afraid; and beginning to sink, he cried, saying, Lord, save me.

And immediately Jesus stretched forth his hand, and caught him, and said unto him, O thou of little faith, wherefore didst thou doubt?

Matthew 14:25-31

Here we see Peter started with faith that was very dynamic and uncommon. He was bold to go to the Lord on the sea. He walked on the sea for a while as long as he had his eyes on the Lord. But he shifted his gaze from the Lord ...***But when he saw the wind boisterous, he was afraid;*** Notice again how fear can rob us of the greatest experience in faith. The point to note is, of what relevance was the contrary wind to his walking on the sea? None! Remember he did walk on it even while it was stormy anyway. The earlier verse of Matthew 14:24 told us so; ***But the ship was now in the midst of the sea, tossed with waves: for the wind was contrary.*** We must watch out here for factors that are both irrelevant and distractive targeted at making us loose the focus of the object of our desire. Hence, we can do great things in faith as long as our eyes are on

Christ. Hebrews 12:2 says *Looking unto Jesus the author and finisher of our faith;*

THE MEASURE OF FAITH

For I say, through the grace given unto me, to every man that is among you, not to think of himself more highly than he ought to think; but to think soberly, according as God hath dealt to every man the measure of faith.

Romans 12:3

Notice from the above that every born-again Christian already has the same quality and quantity of faith deposited in them. Paul said *"to every man among you, ...God hath dealt to every man the measure of faith"*.

The victory to overcome every problem in this world is deposited hereby. This brings us to a place where it becomes necessary for every carrier of "the measure of faith" to learn how to release, increase and develop what we already possess. Imagine a stone on a roof top lying dormant, it appears harmless, and as a matter of fact anyone including a child can step on it. In science it is called potential energy or energy at rest. This is exactly how many Christians relates to the God-kind of faith on the inside of them. However, when the stone is released from the roof top and allowed to fall off from there it gathers momentum and can be deadly should it land on someone's head. As soon as this stone is released from the roof top, the energy is no longer at rest but in motion and that is referred to as kinetic energy. Equally, a parked bus or loaded gun is harmless despite the energy within, but when put in motion it becomes dangerous to anyone standing in its path. Faith must be released for it to be effective in our lives.

We must also recognize that there will be factors which are stationed in or around us for the purpose of paralyzing our faith, we must not allow them. We must learn to rise above them.

RELEASING YOUR FAITH

I have repeatedly said that your best friend is anyone who helps you to release your faith. As long as we refuse to put our faith into use, it remains dormant. God wants us to continually put our faith to practice thereby developing and increasing in it.

Notice whenever you study the bible at home or go to church and hear a teaching or preaching of the word of God, something would happen to you on the inside that makes you want to do (or immediately do) something you never thought possible. Sometimes you find yourself acknowledging, believing and confessing things you didn't before. That is your faith being released.

So then faith cometh by hearing, and hearing by the word of God.

Romans 10:17

The word of God when fed to your spirit or preached in your hearing has the ability to stir you up and propel your faith into active and living faith.

As newborn babes, desire the sincere milk of the word, that ye may grow thereby:

1 Peter 2:2

When God's living word is declared and met with living faith, miracle is inevitable. Our Sunday mornings become supernatural. I have seen people acted on the word of God when they heard it in simple faith and they have experienced tremendous miracles.

Believers must consciously daily walk by faith. This is why we should arm ourselves with God's faith filled word daily and not only on Sundays. As we do this we are ready to combat every opposition by releasing our faith where necessary.

Faith must be put into practice by the hearer to get the benefit of it.

But be ye doers of the word, and not hearers only, deceiving your own selves.

For if any be a hearer of the word, and not a doer, he is like unto a man beholding his natural face in a glass:

For he beholdeth himself, and goeth his way, and straightway forgetteth what manner of man he was.

But whoso looketh into the perfect law of liberty, and continueth therein, he being not a forgetful hearer, but a doer of the work, this man shall be blessed in his deed.

James 1:22-25

Faith is the word of God applied. Simply doing what the word of God says.

When this procedure becomes an established pattern in the believer's life, growth and increase in faith will be experienced.

CHAPTER THREE

THE GREATEST FAITH EVER!

The God-kind of faith is a subject that all must embrace. It is a must for all would-be over comers. The subject of faith is perhaps the most important in the bible.

One of the greatest men of our time once said that "any preacher who is yet to preach it has not preached the bible".

However, this subject is not new. It was demonstrated by patriarchs of old.

Faith generally, is simply confidence or trust in a person: it could also be referred to as total confidence in another's ability.

Faith is the total trust in God and in His promises

as made through Christ and the Scriptures by which humans are justified, saved or delivered.

Now faith is the substance of things hoped for, the evidence of things not seen.

Hebrews 11:1

Faith and hope have a connection. Their intentions are the same. But when faith shows up hope becomes history. Notice ...***substance of things hoped for,*** Faith gives substance to what you hoped for. Faith provides to the eye of the mind the reality of those things that cannot be discerned by the eye of the body.

Faith becomes vital or important because of the following:

It is demanded by the Almighty God...

But without faith it is impossible to please him: for he that cometh to God must believe that he is, and that he is a rewarder of them that diligently seek him.

Hebrews 11:6

It is the only avenue that leads to God's grace...

For by grace are ye saved through faith; and that not of yourselves: it is the gift of God:

Ephesians 2:8

Necessitated by the ferocious assault from the kingdom of darkness...

Above all, taking the shield of faith, wherewith ye shall be able to quench all the fiery darts of the wicked.

Ephesians 6:16

It is the secret of every victor...

For whatsoever is born of God overcometh the world: and this is the victory that overcometh the world, even our faith.

1 John 5:4

It is the assured way of receiving blessings from God...
If any of you lack wisdom, let him ask of God, that giveth to all men liberally, and upbraideth not; and it shall be given him.

But let him ask in faith, nothing wavering. For he that wavereth is like a wave of the sea driven with the wind and tossed.

For let not that man think that he shall receive any thing of the Lord.

James 1:5-7

It is the believer's way of life...

(For we walk by faith, not by sight:)

2 Corinthians 5:7

...but the just shall live by his faith.

Habakkuk 2:4

It is the only fight a believer is permitted to engage in unashamedly...

Fight the good fight of faith, lay hold on eternal life, whereunto thou art also called, and hast professed a good profession before many witnesses.

1 Timothy 6:12

In this chapter I intend to help unravel some of the keys to walking in the greatest faith ever. Needless to say that there were and will be other demonstration of great faith, however, the emphases here are on those particular circumstances sighted by the Lord himself.

I believe it is important to take the whole bible seriously. I know every preacher of God's word teaches this. However, since the subject of faith is of great importance as highlighted above, I believe every statement the Lord made about it should even be more scrutinized.

And when Jesus was entered into Capernaum, there came unto him a centurion, beseeching him,

And saying, Lord, my servant lieth at home sick of the palsy, grievously tormented.

And Jesus saith unto him, I will come and heal him.

The centurion answered and said, Lord, I am not worthy that thou shouldest come under my roof: but speak the word only, and my servant shall be healed.

For I am a man under authority, having soldiers under me: and I say to this man, Go, and he goeth; and to another, Come, and he cometh; and to my servant, Do this, and he doeth it.

When Jesus heard it, he marvelled, and said to them that followed, Verily I say unto you, I have not found so great faith, no, not in Israel.

And I say unto you, That many shall come from the east and west, and shall sit down with Abraham, and Isaac, and Jacob, in the kingdom of heaven.

But the children of the kingdom shall be cast out into outer darkness: there shall be weeping and gnashing of teeth.

And Jesus said unto the centurion, Go thy way; and as thou hast believed, so be it done unto thee. And his servant was healed in the selfsame hour.

Matthew 8:5-13

There are two reasons why this passage should receive much attention;

1. The first thing to observe in this passage that

should get everybody's attention is the fact that Jesus Christ, the Lord himself, was filled with surprise.

When Jesus heard it, he marvelled, I believe whatever got the Lord's attention and amazed Him should get every believer's attention. We must therefore pay attention to what actually transpired. We had this same occasion in Mark 6:6, it was said that the Lord also marveled because of the unbelief of the Jews. However, here comes a Gentile displaying an uncommon reliance or trust in God's ability.

Without doubt, the presence or the absence of faith deeply concerns the Lord and it is a matter of paramount importance to him.

2. ***Verily I say unto you, I have not found so great faith, no, not in Israel.*** This portion of scripture establishes that the Lord has a keen interest in the subject of faith and He is ever watching or searching for it undoubtedly with the purpose of rewarding it.

But watch this second point;

I have not found so great faith, the Lord was emphatic in His comparison of what He had seen expressed by this man to whatever he had experienced throughout Israel. He commended this man's faith.

It reminded Him of what He had always wanted for His own people.

Imagine you spending time coaching and teaching something precious to your own people and while they grapple with it, another comes along from an unlikely source and displayed such a mastery of it.

And I say unto you, That many shall come from the east and west, and shall sit down with Abraham, and Isaac, and Jacob, in the kingdom of heaven.

But the children of the kingdom shall be cast out into outer darkness: there shall be weeping and gnashing of teeth.

Matthew 8:11-12

KEY ELEMENTS

- He Came In Humility.

This man was evidently a man of affluence, an

officer of the army, yet he came in humility. Matthew 8:5 reads ...***there came unto him a centurion, beseeching him,*** he did not come arrogantly demanding attention like some would. But he came begging the Lord. Beseeching means "to beg for urgently".

In verse 6, we read ...***And saying, Lord,*** he further acknowledges Christ as Lord hence attributing power and authority to Him.

The fear of the LORD is the instruction of wisdom; and before honour is humility.

Proverbs 15:33

...and be clothed with humility: for God resisteth the proud, and giveth grace to the humble.

1 Peter 5:5

God has an eye of favour to the humble. The above scripture says he gives more grace to the humble.

So Christ agrees to come to this our friend's home and heal his servant. And then he goes again:

The centurion answered and said, Lord, I am not worthy that thou shouldest come under my roof:

Matthew 8:8

Notice again *"I am not worthy"* the extent of the centurion's humility and apparent self-abasement before Christ. He did not only abase himself he equally esteemed Christ very highly ...***I am not worthy that thou shouldest come under my roof:*** This man totally recognized his inadequacies before the Lord.

*...**Lord, I am not worthy*** this also shows that the centurion did not approach the Lord based on any spiritual or physical credit held by him to which he now seeks benefits but rather he simply trusted that grace will be extended to him. It is possible to be arrogant in prayer without knowing it:

Two men went up into the temple to pray; the one a Pharisee, and the other a publican.

The Pharisee stood and prayed thus with himself, God, I thank thee, that I am not as other men are, extortioners, unjust, adulterers, or even as this publican.

I fast twice in the week, I give tithes of all that I possess.

And the publican, standing afar off, would not lift up so much as his eyes unto heaven, but smote upon his breast, saying, God be merciful to me a sinner.

I tell you, this man went down to his house justified rather than the other: for every one that exalteth himself shall be abased; and he that humbleth himself shall be exalted.

Luke 18:12-14

Notice that great doors of grace and mercy can be opened by humility.

I am reminded of the patriarch Abraham while interceding for Sodom and Gomorrah.

And Abraham answered and said, Behold now, I have taken upon me to speak unto the LORD, which am but dust and ashes:

Genesis 18:27

We can begin to understanding why he got the result of favour. He abased himself acknowledging before God he was but dust and ashes.

To further confirm this truth, let us examine another case the Lord referred to as an exercise of great faith.

And, behold, a woman of Canaan came out of the same coasts, and cried unto him, saying, Have mercy on me, O Lord, thou son of David; my daughter is grievously vexed with a devil.

But he answered her not a word. And his disciples came and besought him, saying, Send her away; for she crieth after us.

But he answered and said, I am not sent but unto the lost sheep of the house of Israel.

Then came she and worshipped him, saying, Lord, help me.

But he answered and said, It is not meet to take the children's bread, and to cast it to dogs.

And she said, Truth, Lord: yet the dogs eat of the crumbs which fall from their masters' table.

Then Jesus answered and said unto her, O woman, great is thy faith: be it unto thee even as thou wilt. And her daughter was made whole from that very hour.

Matthew 15:22-28

From the above scriptures, here we were introduced to another gentile, and again she came like the Roman officer begging for mercy rather than claiming any merit. However, she was treated like we have never read before in Christ's ministry. Totally ignored! Her humiliation just got started, when the Lord was pressured by the disciples to send her away He responded,

I am not sent but unto the lost sheep of the house of Israel. Many people would have lost it at this junction. How she managed to keep her composure is a mystery. To remain calm after been ignored, slighted and snubbed is laudable.

Notice that those that are easily discouraged or easily offended cannot walk this path.

Her response was to worship Him and begged still for help. And as if she had not suffered enough,

Christ further tested her humility: *But he answered and said, It is not meet to take the children's bread, and to cast it to dogs.* At this junction, I know many of us would have given it to Him. Thank God she was not many of us! This woman demonstrated such grace of heart and was without doubt an obvious example worthy of emulation when she answered this seeming reproach and said *...Truth, Lord: yet the dogs eat of the crumbs which fall from their masters' table.*

It is nothing short of ingenuity to calmly come up with sound and a wise response where many would have lost composure. Look again at her response *...yet the dogs eat of the crumbs,* that is, she accepted she was a dog. And as a dog she pleaded for crumbs. What a great lesson we can learn in the attitude of this genius.

Undoubtedly, great faith often utilizes the key of humility to open the precious door of unmerited favour.

- He Understood The Authority of The Word of Christ

...but speak the word only, and my servant shall be healed.

For you to recognize the power behind a man's word you must first know who the man is. This man did not only believe in the Lordship of Christ *...there came unto him a centurion, beseeching him,* **And saying, Lord,** *my servant lieth at home sick of the palsy,* he equally recognized the power of his word. This centurion totally understood authority and how that works from his own background as an officer over his subjects.

...but speak the word only, in other words, just give the instruction, it is finished. Wow! The centurion realized the way his words unquestionably affect his subjects is the way the word of Christ will affect the disease in the body of his servant.

Great faith accepts what the centurion accepted about the word of Christ. This faith knows nothing can challenge the authority of God's word. Great faith simply recognizes that God's word is the final authority over every situation and circumstances of our lives.

God's word is a sure word. It is dependable. It can never fail. It is quick, alive and it can travel any distance.

God Himself said so:

So shall my word be that goeth forth out of my mouth: it shall not return unto me void, but it shall accomplish that which I please, and it shall prosper in the thing whereto I sent it.

Isaiah 55:11

Jesus said the same:

Heaven and earth shall pass away, but my words shall not pass away.

Matthew 24:35

Apostle Peter said you do well to pay attention to God's word:

We have also a more sure word of prophecy; whereunto ye do well that ye take heed, as unto a light that shineth in a dark place, until the day dawn, and the day star arise in your hearts:

2 Peter 1:19

The psalmist said it is settled:

For ever, O LORD, thy word is settled in heaven.

Psalm 119:89

■ Great Faith Perseveres

It is important to note that Great faith does not give up. Many often start the journey with incredible and commendable attitude of faith but are soon dissuaded because of life's challenges. Peter demonstrated one of the most outstanding faith ever recorded in the gospel. No one ever tried to walk on water aside the Master Himself. Peter accepted the word of Christ saying "COME" and he took off. However, upon sighting what appeared to be an opposing force he doubted.

But when he saw the wind boisterous, he was afraid;

Matthew 14:30

The wind had nothing to do with walking on water, furthermore, it was there before he started out on the water.

Strong and great faith will weather the storms of discouragement and make that which seems to be against it work for it.

To persevere means to persist in a state, enterprise, or undertaking in spite of counterinfluences, opposition, or discouragement.

One unique example is the rare woman in Matthew 15 who received the seeming rejection and reproach by Christ without been dissuaded and distracted from what she came for.

Many people's ability to exercise faith has been crushed by reason of offence.

Great faith has an incurable habit of persevering.

Christ gave a solid of example of what persevering is all about.

And he spake a parable unto them to this end, that men ought always to pray, and not to faint;

Saying, There was in a city a judge, which feared not God, neither regarded man:

And there was a widow in that city; and she came unto him, saying, Avenge me of mine adversary.

And he would not for a while: but afterward he said within himself, Though I fear not God, nor regard man;

Yet because this widow troubleth me, I will avenge her, lest by her continual coming she weary me.

And the Lord said, Hear what the unjust judge saith.

And shall not God avenge his own elect, which cry day and night unto him, though he bear long with them?

I tell you that he will avenge them speedily. Nevertheless when the Son of man cometh, shall he find faith on the earth?

Luke 18:1-8

Notice the whole essence of the parable is to dissuade men from giving up. *...he spake a parable unto them to this end,* What end Lord? *...that men ought always to pray, and not to faint;* see that the end is that man must learn to persevere and not give up.

And he would not for a while: Many factors may appear to discourage us and make us abandon our faith but, to get to the end and reap the reward of our faith, we must persevere.

The Lord said this unjust judge was overcome by persistence.

Praise God perseverance has the ability to overcome known and unknown difficulties in our faith walk.

Remember Jesus said also that our righteous God will unfailingly reward our faith when we persevere.

CHAPTER FOUR

THE PROOF OF FAITH

For faith to become effective and produce profit or benefit there must be a corresponding action. The word of God when mixed with faith should lead us into an action which in turn releases the blessings of God over our lives.

Many Christians often claim to have faith but their works or corresponding action does not support such claims.

What doth it profit, my brethren, though a man say he hath faith, and have not works? can faith save him?

If a brother or sister be naked, and destitute of daily food,

And one of you say unto them, Depart in peace, be ye warmed and filled; notwithstanding ye give them not those things which are needful to the body; what doth it profit?

Even so faith, if it hath not works, is dead, being alone.

Yea, a man may say, Thou hast faith, and I have works: shew me thy faith without thy works, and I will shew thee my faith by my works.

Thou believest that there is one God; thou doest well: the devils also believe, and tremble.

But wilt thou know, O vain man, that faith without works is dead?

Was not Abraham our father justified by works, when he had offered Isaac his son upon the altar?

Seest thou how faith wrought with his works, and by works was faith made perfect?

And the scripture was fulfilled which saith, Abraham

believed God, and it was imputed unto him for righteousness: and he was called the Friend of God.

James 2:14-23

James here speaks on the post born-again experience. His letter to already saved brethren reiterates the fact that it is possible for Christians to be deceived into thinking that they are living by faith when it is not so.

But be ye doers of the word, and not hearers only, deceiving your own selves.

James 1:22

Notice that faith is a doer of God's word.

Faith without works or corresponding action is dead.

James says faith is perceivable ...*shew me thy faith without thy works, and I will shew thee my faith by my works.*

We must know to act on the word of God that we believed.

Often we say we have faith in God. We talk about believing God for a new job or finance, yet we are sitting at home anxious for our needs. We say we believe God for our physical health, and yet we cover ourselves up on the bed talking about what the sickness is doing to us. Faith must have corresponding actions. Faith without corresponding action is dead. It's not going to produce anything. It is merely mental assent. You merely say that it's possible, that it's true, but you are not willing to do anything about it, so you do not get the result that it promises.

And they come unto him, bringing one sick of the palsy, which was borne of four.

And when they could not come nigh unto him for the press, they uncovered the roof where he was: and when they had broken it up, they let down the bed wherein the sick of the palsy lay.

When Jesus saw their faith, he said unto the sick of the palsy, Son, thy sins be forgiven thee.

Mark 2:3-5

In verse 5 we read ***...Jesus saw their faith*** what was

it that Jesus saw? He saw their action in breaking through the roof. James said ... ***I will shew thee my faith by my works.*** Faith is not idle, it is a mover, and it sets things in motion.

Faith's corresponding action must be evident in three areas of our lives.

- ❖ In our thinking. Must align with God's word

- ❖ In our confessions. Must not be against God's word

- ❖ In our action. Must do what the word says.

www.ingramcontent.com/pod-product-compliance
Lightning Source LLC
LaVergne TN
LVHW041437170726
843492LV00008B/2661